D

Danny Wallace
and the
Centre of the
Universe

Danny Wallace

EBURY
PRESS

Published in Great Britain by Ebury Press in 2006

1 3 5 7 9 10 8 6 4 2

First published by
Ebury Press
Random House, 20 Vauxhall Bridge Road,
London SW1V 2SA

Random House Australia (Pty) Limited
20 Alfred Street, Milsons Point, Sydney,
New South Wales 2061, Australia

Random House New Zealand Limited
18 Poland Road, Glenfield,
Auckland 10, New Zealand

Random House (Pty) Limited
Isle of Houghton, Corner of Boundary Road & Carse O'Gowrie,
Houghton 2198, South Africa

The Random House Group Limited Reg. No. 954009

www.randomhouse.co.uk

A CIP catalogue record for this book is available from
the British Library

Typeset by SX Composing DTP, Rayleigh, Essex
Cover Design by Two Associates

ISBN 9780091908942 (from Jan 2007)
ISBN 0091908949

Papers used by Ebury Press are natural, recyclable products
made from wood grown in sustainable forests

Printed and bound in Denmark by
Nørhaven Paperback A/S

In Memory of Gold Joinee Cazz

Danny would like to thank . . .

The truly lovely people of Wallace, Idaho – in particular Mayor Ron Garitone, Prime Minister Rick, and of course the fount of all knowledge, Greg Marsh (whose excellent Wallace website you can find at www.wallace-id.com). Cheers!

About the author . . .

Danny Wallace has written several books, including *Join Me* (all about what happened when he started his own cult), and *Yes Man* (all about what happened when he decided to say 'Yes' . . . to *everything*). Both are currently in development for film. He also presents TV shows. His own six-part BBC2 series, *How To Start Your Own Country*, recently saw him become a King. But you might also have caught him on BBC1, SkyOne, Channel 4, or on a chat show in Belgium, where for some reason he is loved. He lives in London, and he says he adores you.

Contents

1 Journey to the centre of the earth

'It was the sound I heard first. There were lights in the sky, and police on the streets . . .

'The sound became deafening and then we saw them . . .

'One marching band. One Mayor. Hundreds of people.

'They all stood around a manhole cover that had been roped off with police tape. The Mayor started to make a speech. He was declaring the manhole to be the Centre of the Universe. The entire town cheered.

'The Mayor explained that since nobody can prove that the manhole *isn't* the Centre of the Universe, then the manhole *must be* the Centre of the Universe.

'And the strangest thing is, it all kind of made sense . . .'

Eyewitness Zurin Trzaska,
a confused tourist passing through town,
25 September 2004

Monday
There are two things you can see very clearly from my window right now.

1

One is the sky. A huge, dark blue sky. And the other is London. Not all of it. Just bits of it. Bits like the Dome. Or the skyscrapers around Docklands. Or this one weird tower, far away. A weird tower that they light up at night, which just sits there – all bright and white, on top of a hill.

For years, I had no idea what that tower was. All I knew was, even on a mucky, cloudy night you could see it, like someone had drawn it on your window in Tipp-Ex.

And then one day I found myself standing right next to that tower. I hadn't meant to. I was up on a hill, miles from home, trying to spot where I lived in the distance. I could see all of London. Well, not all of it. Just bits of it. Bits like the Dome. Or the skyscrapers around Docklands. But I couldn't see that one weird tower, far away. That weird tower they light up at night. The one that just sits there, all bright and white, on top of a hill.

And that was when I looked around.

It turns out I'm in Greenwich. Well, I say 'turns out'. I *know* I am in Greenwich, to be honest. I've gone there on purpose, after all. I've gone there for a number of reasons, in fact. To see a friend. To have a pint. To have a laugh. And now here I am, next to that big tower, with a sign that I can now read for the very first time. The Royal Observatory. Home to the seventh biggest telescope in the world, pointed deep into space. And home also of one of the most famous lines in the world. The line that divides the planet into east and west. The line that tells you you're standing on the very Centre of the Earth.

There are tourists everywhere, jumping over the line and back again. Laughing, and taking pictures of each other. I suppose it's a picture you just *have* to take, like if you're in front of the Eiffel Tower, or the Great Wall of China, or a sea monster. The problem is, a small line on a concrete floor in the middle of a park doesn't look quite as grand. I feel sorry for the tourists who try and impress their friends with their holiday snaps when they get home.

'Look!' they'll say. 'Here I am standing at the Centre of the Earth!'

They will probably tap the photo excitedly at this point.

'Oh,' their friends will say. 'Because it looks

like you're just standing near a park.'

I lean against a wall, shaking my head at this thought and studying the tourists with pity.

And then I get one of them to take my picture kneeling at the Centre of the Earth. And I go home, very happy indeed.

Back at the flat, I impress my girlfriend by pointing out of the window a lot.

'That tower there is part of the Royal Observatory,' I say.

'Yes,' she says. 'You keep telling me that.'

It's true. I do.

'It's where they keep the Centre of the Earth,' I say. 'I didn't know that before, but now I do.'

'You keep telling me that, as well,' she says.

'Yes,' I say, because once again, she is correct.

There is a pause.

'Have I shown you the photo of me at the Centre of the Earth?'

And then I remember that I have. Twice.

I found it quite exciting that I could see the Centre of the Earth from my window. It was now the first thing I looked at in the mornings and the last thing I checked at night. I'm not sure why I felt the need to check. It's not like they'd move the Centre of the Earth somewhere else in the middle of the night – after realising they'd got their sums wrong and it was actually in Kettering. But I loved knowing that, whatever happened, I was close to the centre of things. Close to where everything was balancing. Close to zen. Close to the Centre of the Earth.

And then one night, I made the mistake of looking up.

It was a clear night, and I saw something incredible. Inches away from the perfect circle of the moon, I saw a star. Now, a star isn't something you're used to seeing in London –

not unless it's a soap star, or someone from *The Bill*. When stars get to London, they tend to hide. The lights are too bright, and the sky can't cope. What should be a pitch-black cloak becomes a dull and dark orange. And as I looked at the star, I realised what millions of other people have realised when looking at stars. We're tiny. We don't matter. We're here for a second and then gone the next. We're a sneeze in the life of the universe. But . . . the universe itself – that's a different story. That's been here *forever*. It'll *be* here forever. One day, when the earth is just a rumour, the universe is all that will be left.

Mind you, that's quite a lot.

I felt full of wonder, yet empty and sad too.

So I ate a biscuit and watched an episode of *EastEnders*. And, after a bit, everything was all right again.

The next day, though, something was still playing on my mind. The photo of me kneeling at the Centre of the Earth had become the image on my computer desktop. I started to wonder how many other people had done something similar with theirs. I searched the internet for images. I found dozens of pictures just like mine. Americans standing on the Centre of the Earth. Poles standing on the Centre of the Earth. Japanese, Swiss, Spanish, Koreans . . . All of them doing precisely the same thing as me, with the same silly grins on their faces. All of them feeling important. All of them feeling right at the centre of things. And if we're honest, all of them looking like they're just standing near a park.

It got me thinking about my nearly deep moment of the night before. My deep moment when I'd considered life, the universe and everything. The Centre of the Earth is nothing compared to the Centre of the Universe. I mean, how many more people would get their photos taken at the Centre of the Universe if they could? How many more tourists would flock there in a second if it was possible? To see where life had first begun? To see the very place that had given birth to everything else in the entire world? In the entire *universe?*

So I searched the internet for images of the Centre of the Universe . . . perhaps Neil Armstrong had taken a quick photo of it on his way to the Moon. Maybe the Russians had sent a monkey up there with a camera. But all I found were diagrams, pictures of stars, control rooms, and men with beards pointing at blackboards.

And then I found a sentence that made me realise that searching for images might not quite work: 'Scientists argue that the universe is actually expanding.' Now I *knew* this. Well, I'd heard about it, anyway. But it made me think . . .

The universe is actually expanding! Getting bigger every second! If that's true, then it means the centre must be getting further away from us! Or *we're* getting further away from *it*! Further away with every word you read! And if we *are* getting further away, then the time to leave in order to get there quickly is always right *now*. Right this minute. Right this *moment!*

I thought about how long the universe has had to expand and my head nearly popped. It's had billions and billions of years to expand! Billions and billions of years for the centre to get further and further away! It's probably *miles* away already!

I read on . . . Some scientists reckon that, even if you travelled at the speed of light, it would take longer than any human could live to get

8

there. No wonder there were no pictures of it. How could the flash work if you were travelling at the speed of light? You'd probably just end up with pictures of the back of your own head.

But I kept searching the net. And clicking on links to different websites. And looking at pictures. And reading things I didn't understand. And then, just when I was about to stop and pop the kettle on . . . I found something.

A clue.

Something written on a webpage, a personal webpage, a blog.

Something about *finding* the Centre of the Universe. Not looking for it. But *finding* it.

Something about . . . *Idaho?*

A man named Zurin had been passing through a small town when he'd seen something rather unusual. A ceremony of some kind.

It seems that the mayor of a tiny town tucked away in the valleys of Idaho had found proof that his town wasn't just a tiny town after all. It was an important town. A town we needed to know about. Because that mayor had found proof that his town was in fact . . . the *very Centre of the Universe.*

It was a bold claim. A claim so bold that for a

moment I wasn't sure I could take it all that seriously. In fact I knew I couldn't. Until I saw the name of the town. A name which took my breath away.

It was incredible.

It was a cosmic coincidence.

It was surely . . . a *sign!*

The town which claimed to be the Centre of the Universe . . . had my name.

The town which claimed to be the Centre of the Universe . . . was called *Wallace.*

2 Journey to the centre of the universe

'I, Ron Garitone, Mayor of Wallace, declare this town to be the Centre of the Universe.

'Thanks to newly discovered science, we were able to pinpoint the exact centre within the Centre of the Universe. A manhole cover in the middle of the street.

'And so it is decided. We are the Centre of the Universe.'

Ron Garitone, The Mayor
25 September 2004,
9pm WUT (Wallace Universal Time)

Wednesday
Look. Let's be honest. There was no way in the world I could find out something like that, and then *not* go to Wallace, was there?

I mean, finding out the Centre of the Universe *exists* is one thing. Finding out it's got the same *name* as you is quite another. I suppose it's a bit like meeting God and realising you're wearing the same shoes.

And so, just a few days later, I booked a ticket.

11

A ticket to the Centre of the Universe. It was something I could never get bored of saying.

I leave today.

I will be taking very careful notes as I spend just one day in the Centre of the Universe. I will update them in my journal, which looks a bit like my diary. Hopefully what follows will be of some use to historians of the future, and scientists of the present. Who knows what I will find out in Wallace? I have emailed the Mayor to tell him that I intend to spend one day of no more than 24 hours studying his claim and finding out more about his town.

All I know is this. About a year ago, a mayor called Ron called a meeting. He gathered everyone from his tiny town round and basically said, 'Look, from now on, if anyone asks, we are the Centre of the Universe. OK?' And everyone had nodded and said 'OK.' Apart from one bloke, who'd said, 'I do hope you have the science to back this bold claim up,' to which the Mayor had simply smiled and replied, 'I do.'

I wanted to believe. I wanted to believe that a small town could make itself big. I wanted to believe that Wallace was the Centre of the Universe. I'll be honest – I didn't believe it. But sometimes you've just got to see what happens. So I decided to see what would happen.

But before I decided to leave for Idaho, I had also attempted to tell the people at Greenwich, the Centre of the Earth, about Wallace. You never know. It may have been something that they wanted to find out about for themselves. So I went on the internet, to the Royal Observatory website, and looked at their list of Frequently Asked Questions. I found the following sentence:

Click here if you have a new theory that changes current ideas on the study of space / science / the formation of the Sun and planets . . .

Well, I figured that applied to me. The theory that the universe began not billions of light years away, but in Idaho. That was something I thought changed current ideas quite a bit. So I clicked there, fully expecting a form of some sort for me to fill in. Perhaps then a scientist would ring me back to congratulate me on changing the course of world history. Instead, the screen changed, and I saw this:

Unfortunately the Royal Observatory does not

have the resources to examine the many new theories that are sent to us from around the world.

I made a 'tsk' noise. All I had wanted was for a man with a beard to read my email. An email which would have informed them that a mayor in Idaho was challenging all their research and ideas about the formation of the universe. I email them anyway.

Dear staff of the Royal Observatory,

I see from your website you are low on resources. Well, please do not worry. What I have found out could change all that forever. You may have been wondering where the Centre of the Universe has got to. Well, it turns out it's in Idaho. Maybe if you didn't spend all day staring into space you'd know these things.

I intend to leave soon for Wallace, Idaho, where I will investigate this claim for myself and report back to you using my own resources. It will not cost you a penny.

Here's to history in the making!

Danny Wallace

14

I have checked my email inbox twice, but they have yet to write back. I imagine they are probably alerting the many scientific journals.

The Mayor's claim had better hold up.

When I get to Seattle, I will change planes and fly to a small airport called Spokane.

I can't bloody *wait*.

Thursday, 7.14am

I've had to wait bloody *hours*.

I have finally, *finally* landed at Spokane Airport in Washington State, after long delays, and I am a little confused. Not only am I jet-lagged, but I have just spent the last two hours talking to a man whose job description is 'Ultimate Fighter'. He is competing somewhere in Spokane and has told me exactly what he is going to do to his opponent in quite some detail. It generally involved a lot of punching to the face and ribs.

Still. Everything is about to get better.

I am to be met by the man who runs the hotel I'm staying in over in Wallace. He will drive us to Idaho in his van. His name is Rick and he said, 'You'll know me when you see me. I'm tall.'

I approach at least three tall men, all of whom turn out not to be Rick. One of them turns out to be the Ultimate Fighter I spent two hours listening to on the plane. That is how confused I am. Eventually, though, I find Rick.

He was right. He is tall.

'Mr Wallace!' he says. 'Mr Wallace going to Wallace!'

There is joy in his eyes as he says this. I am going to fit right in.

'So what is the nature of your business in Wallace?' he says as we start to drive.

'I have come from the Centre of the Earth to see the Centre of the Universe!' I say, delighted.

'Well, you've found it!' he says.

It turns out that Rick isn't just the man who

runs the hotel. He is also, he says, the Prime Minister of Wallace. I am deeply impressed. It is not often that a prime minister picks tourists up from the airport in a small van. It would be truly excellent if Tony Blair did that from time to time. Just randomly turn up at airports to collect various tourists and drop them off at their hotels and B&Bs. I tell Rick I may suggest it to him, if we ever meet.

'You should!' says Rick, and he's right.

'So how did you become the Prime Minister?' I ask. 'I imagine there was some complex voting system or something?'

'Well, to be honest, I just started calling myself the Prime Minister, and it kind of caught on.'

'Oh.'

'I do guided tours of Wallace, and the tourists kind of like it.'

Again, I feel it's another tip Tony Blair might like to take on. Guided tours around Britain. Tony in a transit van with nine tourists. From Guildford to Greenock, for months on end.

And then Rick tells me all about Wallace, and what lies ahead.

It turns out that Wallace didn't used to be

called Wallace at all. In 1884, it was called Cedar Swamp, on account of all the cedar trees. And the swamps. Later, it was called Placer Center. That was on account of the small lumps of dirt and mud you get by riverbanks. Neither of these seemed like particularly romantic names.

It was when a man called Colonel W.R. Wallace (who was *not* a colonel) applied to get a post office going that things changed. His wife, Lucy, was put in charge of things. She must have been bored. There were only fourteen people living there. And there are only so many postcards you can send that say 'it's a bit swampy here'.

Lucy clearly didn't like living in a town named after small lumps of dirt. She didn't want to go back to a swampy name, either. So one day, she gathered everyone round. She claimed she'd had a letter from the US Postal Service saying they didn't like the name Placer Center. It was too long. Clearly, she was talking bollocks. There were plenty of places in America with longer names. In 1781, there was a settlement in LA (surely the world's shortest name) with a much longer name. It was called *El Pueblo de Nuestra Senora la Reina de Los Angeles de*

18

Porciuncula. By the time eighteenth-century locals had finished telling people where they lived, it was already 1972.

Still, everybody loved Lucy, and believed her when she said that 'Placer Center' was just too long. So they all came up with suggestions, which were probably just as bad. Names like 'Only Fourteen Of Us Live Here' or 'Hang On, Our Old Name Is *Definitely* Shorter Than That Spanish One'.

But then good old Mrs Wallace had a brainwave. She said, 'Hey . . . why don't we call it *Wallace*? *Wallace* is a good name for a town!' Her husband, the Colonel, blushed and said no. But Lucy ignored him and went ahead and did it anyway. She filled in a form, and Wallace was born.

I only have one question for Rick.

'So why did the Colonel call himself a colonel, if he wasn't a colonel?'

Rick shrugs.

'I don't know.'

'It seems a bit odd to me,' I say.

'Yeah,' says Rick.

And then the Prime Minister and I drive into the small valley where Wallace lies waiting.

3 Journey to the centre of town

8.41am

Good Lord. Wallace is tiny. Absolutely *tiny*. As tiny as a kitten's lips. Tinier, even. That's the first thing you notice. The only thing you can take in at first.

The road, what Americans call the freeway, that we've used to get to Wallace goes all the way from Seattle to Boston. West to East. One long, curving road for days. But at Wallace, things take a slight detour.

'When they started building the freeway, it was supposed to destroy about half of Wallace,' says Rick.

I wonder how you could ever split Wallace in two. It would be like splitting the atom.

'But the locals kept the builders busy with questions for years and years. When they finally got round to trying to build the thing through the town, they saw that the locals had been secretly putting every single building in town onto the Historic Register. That meant they now couldn't touch Wallace, so now the freeway goes *around* Wallace, not through it . . .'

I like that. It's always better when Jerry beats Tom.

I look around.

I have finally arrived at the Centre of the Universe.

8.44am
My hotel is called the Wallace Inn.

'Mr Wallace, staying at the Wallace Inn, in Wallace!' says the lady, checking me in. She seems delighted. I too am delighted. I repeat the same sentence and we both laugh. Although it makes us both sound a bit like simpletons.

'So what have you got planned in Wallace?' she says.

'Nothing, really. I sent an email to the Mayor saying I was on my way, so I should pop round there soon. I'm meeting a bloke called Greg, who's got his own Wallace website. But what else should I do?'

I smile, knowing full well what she'll say. A certain 'galactic landmark', perhaps?

'You could see the site of the only freeway stoplight between Boston and Seattle.'

I'll be honest. It doesn't seem quite as tempting.

'Um . . .'

'You really should.'

'Should I?'

'Yes. When they finished the freeway they said we had to take the stoplight down. It was a sad day.'

'I can imagine,' I say, which is weird, because I can't. 'So . . . what happened? You took the stoplight down?'

'Oh yes. But more than that. The town held a funeral for the stoplight.'

Eh?

'I'm sorry?'

'Yes. We held a funeral for the stoplight. Everyone was there to pay their respects.'

'The town had a funeral? For a *stoplight*?'

'Uh-huh. A nice procession.'

'A nice procession . . . for a *stoplight*?'

I am hoping that by repeating the words 'for a stoplight', the lady might say, 'oh hang on, no – for a *hamster*', but she does not.

'The stoplight, yeah. It's now lying in the old

22

railroad museum. You could take a look at it later.'

I say I will, and do my best to look respectful and grave. This must have been one special stoplight.

And then I ask her if I can have directions to the Mayor's office, instead.

8.47am

As I leave the hotel, I pick up a leaflet. Wallace, it says, was named the *24th Best Place to Buy a Second Home*. I feel that's kind of like getting an award for being 'in' a race, but who am I to judge? I didn't even get nominated. I also realise you don't really need directions in Wallace. If something isn't on one street, it'll probably be on the other one. If it's not on the other one, then someone's probably nicked it.

And, for somewhere claiming to be the Centre of the Universe, it is tiny. If you took a run-up, you could probably jump it. In a valley under a million trees, only 960 people call it home. On the short walk to City Hall, three of them say hello to me. One man waves at me from his car. I pass shops that won't open for another hour. Antique shops mainly. Two shops selling stuffed animals. A computer shop which also does engraving. An 'Athletics Club' which appeared to be just a rowing machine and some trainers in the window. But it's beautiful. Every house and building looks like it's from *Back to the Future*. I feel like I've stepped off the plane and into a town where the local time is the 1950s.

'Hello!' says another man, walking past me at speed.

'Hello!' I say.

Being polite is certainly very central to the Centre of the Universe.

And then, on Cedar Street, I spot an odd museum. In the window is a pair of giant underpants with the words:

HONESTLY – I'VE NEVER BEEN TO WALLACE, IDAHO

I find this a little unusual. A sentence like that on a pair of large pants seems a strange way to promote an otherwise gorgeous town. But as I study the window, I realise something. Something odd. This is a museum about brothels. Brothels with ladies in them. *Wallace* brothels.

Dozens of Wallace brothels. A sign in the window informs me that Wallace is *famous* for its brothels! I can't quite take it in. How many brothels does a town of a thousand people *need?*

I suddenly feel all dirty. Wallace has *tricked* me into feeling dirty! I glance around, making sure no one has seen me, but they have.

'Not open yet,' says the man.

'No. I mean, isn't it? Not that I'm . . . I'm not all that interested in . . . you know . . . I was just . . . looking at the pants.'

Which didn't sound much better, to be honest.

'Be open about eleven,' says the man, walking away.

'Oh, excellent, thank you very much.'

I start to scuttle away, and cross the street. It's just beginning to rain as I see the one thing I've travelled thousands of miles to see.

A small, blue sign reads CENTER OF THE UNIVERSE. An arrow points it out.

My instinct is to run over. Run over and see if it's real. See if I can bathe in the cosmic wonder of the Centre of the Universe. This is why I'm here, after all – this small blue sign and this small round manhole cover! But maybe I should make this moment more special. Maybe I should wait until I've met the Mayor.

8.55am

Oh, sod it. I can't resist it. The lure is too great. Maybe it's something to do with gravity. Maybe there's some kind of cosmic pull. Yes, that must be it. There is a definite cosmic pull in the air. Some would call it rain, but not me. The cosmos is calling out to me, and it would be rude to try and defy the cosmos.

I decide to make a quick stop.

4   Journey to the centre of absolutely everything

8.56am
I, Danny Wallace, am standing on the very
Centre of the Universe. Here, in this small
street, on a rainy autumn morning, in Idaho.

Of course, the Mayor is yet to explain the
complex science behind his claim. To the
untrained eye, yes, I am merely a man standing
in the middle of the street, staring at a manhole
cover. In any other town in the world, I would
be considered an oddball for this. But right
now, if by some incredible twist of fate the
Mayor is somehow correct, I am the only man
standing here. The only man standing at the
Centre of Absolutely Everything.

I look up at the sky, to see if I can see any

stars. But it is 8.56 in the morning and it is raining. To be honest, I have to admit that it doesn't look much like the Centre of the Universe. I have a sneaking suspicion it might just be a manhole cover. But then, how did I expect it to look? I consider the vastness of space and time for a moment, but then a 4X4 nearly runs me over, so I decide to consider it later, over a beer.

9am

'Hello. My name's Danny Wallace. I emailed the Mayor. I've come from the Centre of the Earth.'

I am standing with my back straight and looking proud.

'Oh!' said the lady behind the counter at City Hall.

'Actually,' I say, thinking of something funny, 'I've just come from the Centre of the Universe, which is located about fifty feet from this office!'

I tried to encourage her to laugh at this, but it seemed like she'd heard it before.

'Actually, I've come from London,' I say.

'You have?' says the lady.

'I have,' I say, nodding, which I feel is proof enough.

'I'll just give him a call.'

I take a seat in the narrow corridor while the lady rings the Mayor. I hear a phone ringing, in a room about ten feet away. The phone stops ringing. I hear a man in the other room say 'Hello?'

'I have a Danny Wallace here for you,' says the lady in front of me. 'He's come from the Centre of the Earth.'

There is a pause. And then I hear a man down the corridor quite clearly saying, 'OK, send him through.'

The lady looks at me and says, 'Did you hear that?'

I nod and stand up.

I am going to meet the Mayor.

9.04am

The Mayor is a very enthusiastic man indeed.

'This is so NEAT!' he says, clapping his hands together. 'I LOVE it!'

I smile broadly.

'When I first saw your email, I thought, WHAT? What's a guy from ENGLAND doing

29

coming here to talk to ME for? But this is working out GREAT! I LOVE it! *Your* name is Wallace, the *town's* name is Wallace. You're from the Centre of the *Earth*, we're the Centre of the *Universe*. This is NEAT!'

I like the Mayor a lot. We're getting on like a house on fire.

'Do you mind if I call the press?' he suddenly says.

I wave my hand, and say 'not at all', as if it's a request I hear every time I meet someone new.

He grabs the phone and dials a number.

'Leila? This is Ron Garitone over in Wallace. How busy are you?'

I hear Leila say, 'Well . . . uh . . . not *very*.'

'I have a gentleman here from England, a very interesting young fellow with a strange story. I think you would enjoy him tremendously.'

I am slightly embarrassed. No one has ever enjoyed me tremendously before. But that seems to be all Leila needs to hear. She will send a journalist over to meet me in an hour.

'It's Mr Wallace, staying at the Wallace Inn, in Wallace,' says Ron. 'Now you should be able to remember that, right?'

There is a pause.

'The Wallace Inn,' says Ron. 'Yes . . . that's right.'

He rolls his eyes.

'Wallace, yes. OK! See you later!'

He slams the phone down.

'GREAT!' he says.

'Great!' I say.

'GREAT!' he says.

9.10am

'So,' I say, cutting to the chase. 'You're the man who declared Wallace to be the Centre of the Universe!'

The Mayor looks quite proud. I don't blame him.

'I saw it outside!' I say. 'That must have been a great night!'

'It was,' says Ron. 'It was a wonderful evening. It was a year ago. We got that manhole cover made and put it over the sewer and I made a speech. The paper published it. In *full!*'

'Were the people happy?'

'Very happy. Very happy to be at the Centre of the Universe.'

'And you can prove it, can't you?' I ask.

31

'Because I saw it, and although it looks just like a manhole cover on a road, I read that you can prove beyond all doubt that Wallace is the Centre of the Universe.'

The Mayor looks slightly less sure.

'Well, we base our claim on a very special *type* of science.'

I lean forward, ready to learn.

'Excellent,' I say. 'Fire away.'

'Well . . .' says the Mayor, 'you see, the universe is constantly moving.'

I nod.

'It's constantly growing.'

'Expanding!' I say, pleased to be able to chip in.

'Expanding, yes,' says the Mayor, 'the universe is expanding.'

He leans towards me.

'Now, no one,' he says, with a little point of his finger, 'and I mean *no one* . . . seems to be able to prove exactly *where* the centre is.'

This is all good stuff. And this must be where the science bit comes into it. I make sure I am paying full attention.

'So *we* are proposing . . .' says the Mayor, 'that it's *here*.'

I nod.

The Mayor smiles.

There is a silence.

He sits back.

There is another silence.

I raise my eyebrows, willing him on.

He raises his eyebrows and shrugs.

I don't understand.

Is that *it?*

It can't be!

Did I fall asleep and miss the middle bit? Has *nothing* changed since school?

I am sure there must be more to this science, but from everything that's happening right now in this office in Idaho, there really doesn't seem to be.

'So . . . run me through that again,' I say, although I'm pretty sure I understood it. 'No one knows where the middle of everything that exists is, so the people of Wallace are saying . . .'

'That it's *here*,' says the Mayor, and he taps his desk.

'And . . . that's that?' I say. 'That's the only . . . *proof?*'

I had been hoping for maps, and graphs, and maybe an assistant with a blackboard. I had

33

come a long way today. I *deserved* maps and graphs and an assistant with a blackboard. What was I going to tell the people at the Royal Observatory? They work for the *Queen!* What was I going to tell the *Queen?*

'That's that,' he says. 'You see, what we're saying is this. If you can't prove that this is *not* the Centre of the Universe, then that proves that it *is*. You see?'

I shook my head. I didn't see. The Mayor continued.

'No one can prove that Wallace is *not* the Centre of the Universe. And that means that it *must* be.'

'But I could say, this is *not* the Centre of the Universe, and you can't prove that it *is*!'

'But you didn't say that. And I would say you can't prove that it is *not*, so that *proves* that it is.'

I imagine I looked a little sad at this point, because the Mayor sighed, and then said, 'To be honest, it's just a bit of fun.'

9.14am
Whatever the doubtful science behind it, Ron loves being the Mayor of the Centre of the Universe. And I love him for that.

'The other mayors in the county . . . they get a kick out of it too. I make my speeches about the importance of Wallace, and they like that. We decided that we were the Centre of the Universe, because . . . well, why not? It's something that makes us unique. It separates us. Gives us a different identity from the other towns round here.'

'Do you like living here?' I say.

'Sure I do! This is the same place it was forty years ago when I moved here. This is such a happy town. Everyone knows each other. It's friendly. We don't have the hustle and bustle of the city.'

'You certainly don't,' I say. 'I have seen neither hustle nor bustle, in any order.'

'Don't get me wrong. Cities are great. It's fun to visit them. Why, my wife is going to visit one only this month. But it's not for us. We don't want any of that. There will never be a McDonald's in Wallace. Or a Starbucks. Now, that can cause trouble, of course. Some people *want* a McDonald's hamburger from time to time. But there is a McDonald's just six miles away for that kind of thing.'

I don't want to say it, but the Mayor has just

made me really want a McDonald's hamburger.

'There's no crime here, either,' says Ron.

'None?' I say. Maybe *this* was why Wallace was the Centre of the Universe. Maybe the science doesn't even have to come into it! 'No crime at *all*?'

'Well . . . from time to time someone passes a bad cheque. Or we had a little vandalism recently. And of course we had our . . . "free and easy" times . . .'

Aha. The brothels. The brothels that have their own museum! I gave the Mayor a say-no-more face.

'We probably had fifteen or so "taverns" at one point,' he said, and I could tell that 'taverns' was his way of putting it politely. 'When Wallace was a lot bigger. Yeah, probably fifteen taverns and ten churches. But things have changed since then. We're a town where very little bad happens. This is a town where no one locks their door. No one.'

'What was the last big crime?' I ask.

Ron sits back in his chair and thinks.

'Well, a few years ago they found a skeleton in a chimney. They never did find out who that guy was.'

I was impressed.

'In London, that happens in most *houses*,' I say.

The Mayor looks very serious for a moment.

'Well, it only happened here *once*.'

I nod, gravely.

'And is that another reason why you think Wallace is the Centre of the Universe?' I was trying to look at things with my philosophy hat on. 'The lack of crime? The politeness?'

'Absolutely!' he says. 'We have something special here. Something unique. Why *shouldn't* we be the Centre of the Universe?'

I nod. And then Ron leans forward.

'What's the name of that little town you're from?' he says.

'London,' I say.

'No, the Centre of the Earth thing—'

'Oh. Greenwich. You can see it from my window.'

'And what's Greenwich like?'

'It's very nice.'

'Anything like Wallace?'

'Well, I wouldn't say that . . . It has a Starbucks, for a start.'

Ron looks like he's thinking about

something. He's got a busy day ahead, but he tells me he wants to meet up with me a little later on. He has an idea he thinks I might like.

5 Journey back to the centre of the universe

9.51am

I walk back towards the Centre of the Universe and study it some more. Since meeting the Mayor, it looks more like a manhole cover than it did half an hour ago. It actually just looks like a manhole cover with some writing on it. But maybe I am missing the point. Maybe the manhole cover is just a symbol – maybe the *rest* of Wallace is where I'll find the Centre of the Universe. I decide to explore some more. I'm not here long. I should make the most of it.

10.04am

I've got talking to a man named Joseph, who's lived in Wallace most of his life. A man who admits he's never really left it for long. He also doesn't seem particularly bothered whether it's the Centre of the Universe or not.

'I guess it could be, but so what?' he says. 'Wallace is just where I live. Things used to be better here. Busier. Best place to be. There were thousands of people here. Now there's just a few hundred.'

'Where did everyone go?'

'They followed the money. In '87, the mines around here took a dive. Silver prices went rock bottom. No one had a job any more. You could go from earning fifty thousand a year to nothing. There was a lot of hurt people. People would just drop the keys to their house off at the bank and say "bye".'

'So how do people survive now?'

'We had to look at what else we got. And we got hills. So ski hills became our thing. We get a lot of tourists sometimes for that. We have a law here that says you can drive a snowmobile anywhere in town you like. And then there are other things.'

He points at a building opposite.

'We have twenty people employed across the street there to do something on a computer.'

'What are they doing?'

He shook his head. 'I have no idea.'

I feel sorry for Joseph. Clearly, I am twenty years too late for Wallace's Golden Age.

'Well, maybe so,' says Joseph. 'But some

magazine gave us an award.'

'*Twenty-fourth Best Place to Buy a Second Home?*' I say.

'No, no. Another one. Said we were the Best City in Idaho. That made us kind of proud. But it's not like it was.'

10.30am

I realise that apart from talking to old men on street corners, there is another way to find the beating heart of a town. The local paper! The same local paper I am about to do an interview for! I sit outside a small café and read it. There doesn't seem to be much happening around here. The front page headline reads: SMALL FIRE UNDER INVESTIGATION. Apparently, there was a small fire here last week which is now under investigation. That's pretty much the whole story. Trained men are standing around a small burn mark scratching their heads and wondering what happened. I wonder if they will ever solve the case. Perhaps I could help. I could buy a magnifying glass.

There are only about two pages of news. The rest is who's died this week, and page after page of small ads.

41

> FREE CAR! Brown 1988 Chrysler LeBaron!
> Does not work, probably never will.

I kick myself for not living in Wallace. I could have had a free, broken car!

> Found in Wallace two weeks ago: small
> female Australian shepherd.

I can only hope that this is a type of dog, and not an actual small female Australian shepherd. It would be terrible if it was. How did she get all the way to Wallace? Maybe she was following a sheep and accidentally got on a ferry. But where's the sheep gone? Surely that's a better story than a small fire under investigation.

I have to head back to the Wallace Inn. I have to meet the local journalist who wants to meet me because I am tremendously enjoyable. I imagine the headline. TREMENDOUSLY ENJOYABLE MAN IN TOWN. But with Wallace's history, they would probably assume I was offering some kind of visiting brothel service.

I must remember to ask her if there is any news on the small shepherd.

10.50am

On my way back into the Wallace Inn for my important interview, a rattling blue pick-up truck suddenly stops beside me. A shortish man in a baseball cap jumps out. He looks at me. I look at him.

'Are you Danny?' he says.

I am slightly surprised. I have no idea who this man is.

'Er . . . yes,' I say.

'Danny Wallace?' he says.

'The very same,' I say, which I've never in my life said before, and which makes me sound like something out of the 1800s.

'I thought you must be him. I saw you walking down the road earlier on, and I thought, who the hell is that? Who the hell is that guy? I never seen that guy before, who the hell is he? And then I saw the Mayor and I said I seen you. And I said who the hell was that guy? And he said, well that must've been Danny Wallace. And it was!'

'Yes!' I say, happy to help. 'It was!'

'Well, all I wanted to do was give you a small gift. It's nothin' much. Just something I think you should have. Something to remember us by.'

And with that, he reaches into his pocket and pulls out a coin.

I look at it. I don't know what to say.

'It's a coin,' he says.

Maybe I'd been looking at it too long. No one's ever needed to tell me what a coin looks like before.

'I'm just . . . surprised. And thankful,' I say. 'That's so nice of you!'

I like Wallace more every minute.

10.55am

'Mr Wallace, staying at the Wallace Inn, in Wallace!' says the journalist who's been sent to meet me. She looks delighted at the sentence.

'That's me!' I say, and I try and look delighted too. Although to be honest it has lost some of its impact. But then I remember that I am supposed to be tremendously enjoyable, and so I grin widely.

'So . . . I'm told you're here from England. Why?'

'I wanted to see the Centre of the Universe!' I say. 'Because I'm from the Centre of the Earth!'

'You mean, like the core of the earth?'

'Um . . . no. I mean London.'

'London is the Centre of the Earth?'

'Well, no, Greenwich is.'

'And you're from Greenwich?'

'Actually, no. I live in Bow, which is near Greenwich.'

'So you're from Bow?'

'Well, technically, no. Not "from" Bow, but I do live there. Now. I didn't before. But you can see Greenwich from my window. Well, a tower in Greenwich. At night, anyway.'

The journalist stopped taking notes about halfway into this conversation. But then I remembered something.

'But my last name is Wallace!' I said. 'You know – like the town.'

'Yes,' she said. 'So is that a very unusual name over there?'

Sigh.

'Um. No. Not really.'

I could tell I wasn't being tremendously enjoyable.

'But for a *first* name it is. *Quite* unusual, anyway.'

'But *your* first name is—'

'Danny, yeah.'

11.11am

The interview has started to go better. I think that Erika likes the fact that it took me half a day to get here. I have a feeling the story will revolve more around my flight time rather than my galactic quest.

I try a new angle.

'Of course, in a way I'm here on behalf of the Queen,' I say.

Erika looks like she doesn't believe me.

'What I mean is, she manages the Royal Observatory. Not on a day-to-day basis. She takes more of a backseat role. But I am here in a sense on behalf of the Royal Observatory. In that I sent them an email about the trip and its importance.'

'And what did they say in response?'

I just nodded. And then I pointed at the door and said, 'So maybe we should go and see that manhole again?'

11.26 am
Erika has taken me back to the Centre of the Universe, where she takes my picture. I imagine this will be a story they now stick on page 19, after the deaths and small ads. Or perhaps it will be a tabloid scandal. TREMENDOUSLY ENJOYABLE MAN NOT QUITE SO ENJOYABLE WHEN YOU MEET HIM, ACTUALLY.

It is still raining. I find out that Wallace has its own weather system. This could be a *good*

thing, I think. But then I learn that the fact that it's stuck in a narrow valley means that it rains more in Wallace than anywhere else in Idaho. This is *not* a good thing.

11.45am
'Danny!'

I turn around. It is the Mayor. I am about fifty yards from the manhole cover and he joins me.

'I have a proposal for you,' he says.

'Really?' I say. 'What is it?'

'How would you like to be . . . the official Ambassador to the Centre of the Universe?'

I took a slight step back. And then I realised it looked odd so I took a slight step forward again.

'How do you mean?'

'I mean, how would you like to be the ambassador from Greenwich to the Centre of the Universe?'

I didn't know what to say. This was incredible news!

'Here's what I propose,' says Ron. 'At the next council meeting, I will put you forward for the post. I'll make it official. Absolutely official. I'm gonna give you one of my cards. You give me your phone numbers and we'll make this happen! This is gonna be so NEAT!'

'It is!' I say. 'This is gonna be NEAT!'

I don't know why I felt the need to say NEAT. The Mayor was being so kind to me that I think I felt I should do something kind back.

'This is gonna be FUN!' he says. 'My friend, you'll be hearing from me. This has made my day! Made my WEEK! I had the idea when we were speaking, but I developed it. This is gonna be FUN!'

And it was! I couldn't believe it! I had arrived in Wallace a stranger. I would leave as a fully developed Ambassador!

'And hey, we can make this better!' says Ron, suddenly even more excited. 'How about this. Do you think you can come back next year?'

'Er ... I don't know ... I *guess* so ...' I say.

'GREAT! We'll make it a Danny Wallace Day! A public holiday in your honour! We'll have speeches, and hey! We'll give you the keys to the city! The whole nine yards!'

Bloody hell!

'So what do you say?'

Well, what *do* you say, when the Mayor of a town with your name offers you the key to the place and your own public holiday?

You say, 'Yes! I mean . . . *seriously?*'

This would be the first public holiday ever declared in my honour! Apart from the International Celebration of Daniel Day. But I was nine when I made that up and I'll be honest – it never really took off.

'Yes, seriously! We're gonna make this happen! Danny Wallace Day! Give me all your data – everything! Phone, fax, the works. If I need to call you, I'll call you! I'm serious! Oh golly, I can't wait!'

I was so excited even *I* would've said 'golly'.

The Mayor and I shook hands and then he bounded off.

At last! I am going to have my own public holiday!

6 Keys to the city at the centre of the universe

12.03pm

I have just realised I will probably need a new key-ring for the key to the city. Still, Wallace is quite a small place, so I imagine the key won't be too big. All the same, these are the expenses you never think about when someone gives you

a gift. Perhaps it will come with a key-ring. I will ask when the Mayor phones up.

Lunch, I think!

12.10pm

I am sitting in a pizza place eating an enormous pizza. It is my gift to myself for becoming an ambassador. There's a big screen TV in front of me which is showing Ladies' Snooker. One of the women is wearing trousers so high she could keep a breast in each pocket. A breast in each *trouser* pocket, I mean, not a breast in each *snooker* pocket. If she could keep a breast in each *snooker* pocket, she would have to have *six* breasts, and although steroids could probably make this happen, I don't think Ladies' Snooker has much of a drugs scene yet.

12.30pm

I have finished my pizza.

12.32pm

Anyway, where would you keep six breasts? You'd look a bit odd with six breasts. Like the underside of a cow. Actually, if you had six breasts, it would probably make sense to keep four of them in your pockets, so that no one suspected. That is probably what has happened here. These are the kinds of issues I will probably get to raise in my annual Ambassador's Speech.

I want another pizza.

12.35pm
I have started thinking again about Danny Wallace Day. Perhaps if it catches on, it could become a national thing. Maybe they could introduce it in all the schools in America. Maybe one day, every child in America would start their day by singing a little song about me. Maybe they'd all have to wear little glasses and comb their hair into mullets. God, Danny Wallace Day is going to be brilliant.

12.41pm
Thought about ordering another pizza. But then a man walked in who looked like he had six breasts. I decided I'd probably better not.

12.44pm
A leaflet I picked up in the pizza place has just informed me that my suspicions were correct.

Prostitutes once *ruled* Wallace. The leaflet is for the Oasis Bordello Museum. Bordello seems to be the polite way of saying brothel, but just makes it sound like a car. The new Fiat Bordello.

The Oasis seems to have been the last brothel in town. There used to be one called the Lux, one called the Jade Rooms, and another called the U&I Rooms. That last one is a brilliant name. People don't often credit prostitutes for their wordplay and puns.

On the back of the leaflet were some quotes from happy visitors. Visitors to the museum, obviously, not to the prostitutes.

'Laura was well informed of the history and usage of the bordello. Very enjoyable.'

– The Palmers, Bakersfield, California

I was pleased that the Palmers had found their visit to the brothel very enjoyable, but who were they? Who was Laura? Why was only Laura well informed as to the history and usage? What about the rest of the Palmers? Why did they know so much about the inner workings of a place like that? Why were they so keen to teach Laura this stuff? My mum and dad only ever took me to a museum about how the Post Office works.

'Very informative and excellent tour. Both verbal and visual reminders of what this profession and world really were to those who only looked from the outside in.'

— *The Gibsons, Bakersfield, California*

Hang on . . . *another* family outing from Bakersfield? What was going on in Bakersfield? Why were so many people from Bakersfield interested in brothels? Why were the Gibsons saying it was a good 'reminder'? After all, they were also claiming they only ever looked from the outside in! What were the Gibsons hiding? And did the Palmers know? I hope by pointing this out, I am not going to create some kind of rift between them.

I intend to visit the museum a little later on. I hope I enjoy it as much as the Palmers and the Gibsons. (Who, if you ask me, seemed to enjoy it a little *too* much.)

12.53pm
There is no litter in Wallace. The only piece of

litter I have found so far has been a tiny sliver of chewing-gum wrapper. I am sure this can be sorted, however. When I am Ambassador I will clean up this town.

I see a man with a hammer, banging on the side of a house. I assume he is supposed to be doing this. I say hello and we chat for a little while. And then I ask him what the Centre of the Universe means to him. I mean the manhole cover. He thinks for a second, and then slowly says, 'Friends.'

7 Love and friendship at the centre of the universe

12.56pm
The man has made me think. I loved his answer. I will ask others the same.

1.21pm
The pizza has made me tired. I decide to have a sit down, and walk into a bar called Metals. It is impossible to see through the windows of Metals. As soon as I walk in, I realise I should probably have taken this as a clue. The bar is busy, and as I enter, a dozen men and women turn and look at me. There is no music playing, but if there had been, it would have stopped there and then. There is no talking. I can't turn around and leave. So I walk up to the bar and ask for a lemonade. At least one man frowns.

'Actually,' I say, 'sod it, a shandy.'

I somehow think this will make me fit in more.

'I'm sorry, a what? A *shaddy*?' says the lady behind the bar.

I am now drawing even more attention to myself.

'What's a *shaddy*?'

'A pint of beer, I mean,' I say. 'A pint of beer, please.'

She starts to fill a glass and I notice that all the men here are wearing the same uniform. Baseball cap, checked shirt, five-day stubble, Marlboro Reds, bottle of beer, whisky chaser. She gives me my beer and I go and sit in a corner. Suddenly the conversation starts up again.

'Some guy tried to convince me I need GPS in my truck,' said the man furthest away from the window. 'I told him, why the hell would I need that? I know which mountain I need to be at. And I know that when my ears pop, I'm there.'

It's only mid October, but I find myself sharing a table with a huge Hallowe'en pumpkin and a tiny witch. There's also a ghost dangling above me which keeps very gently hitting my ear. I keep having to bash it away, and it keeps just bouncing back. The harder I bash it, the more attracted it seems to my ears.

I realise I look mental. I drink half my beer and I leave.

1.41pm
I am back at the hotel. I have just changed clothes. Thankfully, I have brought with me a cowboy-style shirt that has just come into fashion in London. It has never gone out of fashion here. I also have a green, army-style jacket. I imagine it makes me look a bit like a hunter. I put both on.

I realise it doesn't make me look like a hunter. It makes me look like someone who can't decide whether they're a redneck or a squaddie. However, I have a slight mullet haircut, which I try and make more obvious. I also decide not to shave today. Now the people of Wallace will definitely have to accept me as one of their own.

1.51pm
I have just walked past the bank and noticed a big colourful sign in the window. It says IT'S CHRIS'S BIRTHDAY! COME IN AND WISH HIM A GOOD DAY! I decide that that is exactly what I will do. It would be a nice gesture. Something to help me make friends with the people of Wallace.

59

But maybe I should get him a present first.

1.59pm
I am in one of the million antique shops in
Wallace, looking for a present for Chris. Oddly
for an antiques shop, there would seem to be no
antiques. I suppose this is a problem when your
country is only about as old as Lionel Blair. All
I can find are stuffed animals (a bear and a
beaver), a photo of Marilyn Monroe sitting on a
swing, and the kind of mug you get free from an
Esso station. None of these seems all that
suitable. It would seem odd walking into the
bank to meet a stranger called Chris and saying
'Happy birthday! I bought you a massive bear!'
In the end, the closest thing I can find to an
antique is a Dean Martin record, called 'I'd Cry
Like a Baby'. I buy it. But first, I ask the man
behind the counter what the centre of his
universe is.

'My family.'

2.07pm
I have just walked up to a complete stranger
and given him a record called 'I'd Cry Like a
Baby'.

'Is Chris in?' I'd said, to a lady wearing glasses and some food on her top.

'He should be over there,' she'd replied, pointing towards the other side of the bank, but I couldn't quite see where she meant. 'He's the guy with the brown hair, quite tall, friendly-looking. He's got a white shirt on, and a tie, I think. And you'll know him because on his desk there's a sign that says "Chris".'

I found him pretty quickly after that.

'Chris!' I said, striding up to him. 'I'm from London! It's your birthday and I thought I would wish you a good day!'

Chris looked a little surprised, and stood up to shake my hand.

'Well, thank you, stranger!' he said, which I thought was pretty cool, because it sounded like something out of a film.

'I also brought you a present!'

'You did?'

'Yes!' I said. 'Here . . .'

I handed him the blue plastic bag which contained his hit record.

'Wow . . .' he said. 'Dean Martin!'

'It's an antique!' I said. 'It dates from as far back as 1954!'

If there's one thing that impresses Americans, it's sentences like that. Chris was clearly impressed, because he just nodded his head and said nothing at all.

'Do you like Dean Martin?'

Chris just kind of nodded again. But it was a weird nod, because it actually looked more like he was shaking his head. I put this down to his being stunned at holding in his hands a real-life antique from the 1950s.

'I hope you've got a record player,' I said.

'Ha ha,' he said, 'well, thank you again!'

I gave him a thumbs-up and left.

2.12pm

I have just realised that Chris didn't actually say if he liked Dean Martin or owned a record player. What if he neither liked Dean Martin nor owned a record player? Still – it's an antique, which dates back as far as 1954. So I am sure it will hold its $5 value in years to come. He could put it in a trust fund. That's £2.50 he never has to worry about again.

Maybe I should have got him the massive bear.

2.38pm

I drop by City Hall again to leave a piece of paper with my contact details on for the Mayor. If Danny Wallace Day is to become a reality, he will need to know how to tell me.

'Oh! You're back!' says the lady behind the counter. 'That's good! That's good! Because I have something for you!'

'Do you?' I say, slightly taken aback.

'Yes!'

'What is it?'

'It's a coin!'

She hands it to me. A coin! My second in a day! From a complete stranger! And it's different from the first!

'Thank you!' I say. 'Thank you so much for my coin!'

3.06pm

It is very weird but satisfying walking through a town which uses your name quite so much. I find myself passing signs for Wallace Antiques, the Wallace Corner Store, the Wallace Fire Department. Then there's the Wallace Inn, the Old Wallace Museum, Wallace Vintage Games. I imagine it would make old Colonel W.R. Wallace extremely proud indeed. And boost his ego too. If it didn't, he'd have some serious self-worth issues. Mind you, he was a bloke who used to wander about calling himself a colonel. So I suppose he probably had some of those anyway.

I am suddenly proud to be the only Wallace wandering around Wallace today. In many ways, that makes me a kind of super-visitor. Someone who *belongs* in Wallace. Much more than that man who works in the bakery. Or that woman behind the till in the garage. I look upon them with pity. Imagine how much better their life would be, living in Wallace, if *they* were a Wallace like me.

Then I realise that I should probably stop thinking things like that. After all, that was how the Nazis started. It would be terrible if I returned to Britain a Nazi. What would my friends say? I decide to fight it. Later, I am seeing the man who does the Wallace website, Greg Marsh. When I see him, I will reassure him by saying, 'I know I'm a Wallace and you're a Marsh and not a Wallace. But that doesn't make me better than you.' It will probably mean a lot. We will both know that I am lying, but it doesn't make it any less nice.

I find out that for the lady who is walking past the computers and engraving shop, the Centre of the Universe is her son.

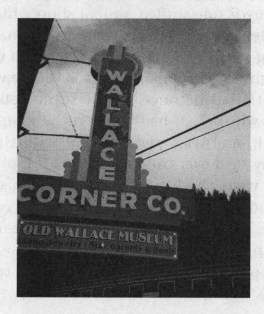

3.17pm
It has stopped raining.

3.18pm
It has started raining again.

3.44pm
Wallace seems to do a roaring trade in stuffed animals. Which is ironic, given that nothing has roared in this town for years. As well as the bear and the beaver I considered for Chris, I have seen dozens of others in shop windows.

There is one stuffed animal shop which also doubles as a pawn shop. I saw an old man with a long beard looking sadly at a stuffed cougar. But why was he looking so sad? Did he want to buy it? Had he once sold it so he could buy more whisky? Or had he been the man who'd shot it, and was now reunited with the only enemy he'd ever truly respected? It looked like they were sharing a moment so I stepped around him and walked towards the counter. There, another old man with a beard was offering $3 for a gun scope.

'Nope,' said the man behind the counter. 'Sorry.'

'Well, I tried my best,' said the other man. '$3. That's my final offer.'

Blimey. What can his *first* offer have been, if that was his *final* one? A hug?

I leave the shop, passing the first old man again, who is now looking sadly at a guitar. I think he just has a sad face. Unless he'd also been enemies with that guitar.

3.57pm

I am looking at the email I received from Greg Marsh. I'd emailed him to ask him how I could get in touch with the Mayor, after finding his website. Greg said he'd make me a cup of tea if I felt like popping round. He'd also given me detailed instructions on how to find him.

> If it is dark out, stand on the Centre of the Universe facing south. Look up. My office is the one with the light on.

I faced south and looked up, but it wasn't dark yet. No matter. He had known that this might happen.

If it is daylight, stop the first person you see and ask, 'Have you seen Greg?'

I stop the first person I see.

'Have you seen Greg?' I ask.

4.06pm

'You see, Wallace wasn't always like this,' says Greg, an instantly likeable man with huge enthusiasm. 'When you left town in the Seventies, there was a huge billboard on the side of the road. It had a giant skull and crossbones on it.'

'No!' I say. *'Pirates?'*

To be honest, it was a long shot.

'Worse,' says Greg. 'Because underneath the skull and crossbones were the words TOUCHING OR DRINKING THE WATER IN THIS VALLEY MAY BE HARMFUL OR FATAL.'

'Even just *touching* the water? Why?'

'Mining. Mining made this whole area like the valley of the damned. As you got towards the next town, you'd notice that nothing was growing. Nothing. No trees. No bushes. The next town usually had this black cloud over it. There was a huge mountain of black slag. These were the "good old days", according to some. I think it was more like hell on earth.

'When I came back twenty years later, I was amazed. Two million trees had been planted. Fish were returning to the river. The river used to be this milky white and now it was pure again. The economy was in the toilet, yes. The silver market had gone, and thousands lost their jobs. But this area was *beautiful* again. People will tell you that the Seventies were the good old days. But how could they be? How can they be the good old days, when to drink the water could kill you?'

Greg is a bearded and slightly untidy gent, but makes hugely comfortable and happy company. He looks like your favourite teacher in the world. A kind of nutty professor – though I suppose that's almost exactly what he is.

'I spent seventeen years looking at the science of dwarf watermelons,' he says. I'm not sure whether he's joking. 'And newborn urine. And biological threat agents. But I decided I'd had enough of all that, but I'd never done enough skiing. So you know what I did? I took a risk. I moved thousands of miles and bought a house for cash on the edge of a forest.'

The idea was to set up a business. But Greg found being a businessman hard. Harder than studying dwarf watermelons, at any rate.

'Poverty set in,' he said. 'But that was a good thing for me. I'm fifty-eight, and in the best shape of my life. I walk four miles a day and I do hard manual labour most of the year. This, for me, is a little piece of paradise.'

Suddenly, he changes the subject.

'I've been wearing this same shirt for ten days now,' he says. 'It's got silver sewn into it, which should eliminate any bad odour.'

I nod but I don't want to get too close in case he asks me to check.

8 Heaven and hell at the centre of the universe

4.20pm

I'm going to meet Greg again in a little while. I think about how strange it is that both he and Joseph were describing the same Wallace earlier. One man thought it was the best place in the world in the Seventies. The other thought it was hell on earth.

He has suggested I visit a place called the Old Smokehouse if I fancy watching Wallace go by, or the 1313 Club. I head off towards Cedar Street to do just that. But I walk past another antique shop, and I spot something in the window. A framed poster, celebrating Wallace's 75th Anniversary. A bearded cowboy on a mule cheerfully throws money about, while the words 'Slippery Gulch' and 'Mammoth Parade' are the only attractions mentioned. I don't know what a slippery gulch is. And I've no idea *where* they were going to find enough mammoths for an entire bloody *parade*. But I

decide that the poster will make a fitting
souvenir of my twenty-four hours there. Along
with both my coins, of course. I go inside.

4.22pm

I have bought the poster. The man was a little
surprised that I was there at all.

'Tourist season is kind of over,' he said.
'Where are you from?'

'I'm from London,' I said.

'You just passing through?'

'No. I came just to see Wallace. I'm going
again tomorrow.'

'Really? Why?'

I handed him my credit card.

'Oh! You're a Wallace!' he said, clearly
delighted. 'In that case I don't mind you buying

this poster.'

'Does it mean a lot to you?'

'I was there on the day of the Silver Jubilee. It's one of my earliest memories. I was eight.'

'Wow. You must've *loved* seeing all the mammoths!'

The man just kind of looked at me. I cleared my throat.

'So is that where you bought the poster?'

'No. I got it on eBay.'

'Oh.'

'But it was a great day. Wallace was a different place back then, of course. Hey . . . if you're a proper Wallace . . . I've got something for you . . . something I *did* get on the day . . .'

He disappeared through a door for a second, and then reappeared, holding something small in his hand.

'It's a coin!' he said.

4.37pm
It has stopped raining.

4.38pm
It has started raining again.

4.40pm
'Everything in this bar is here because of a gun. Look . . . that moose.'

I am hiding from the rain in the 1313 Club on Cedar Street. Eric, a man for whom the Centre of the Universe is 'a beer and a gun', is making me look at a dead moose.

'Now look at that elk, there, look at that. And that bear.'

I look at the elk and then at the bear.

'That beaver.'

I try to look at the beaver. I can't see the beaver.

'Which beaver?'

'That beaver, over there.'

I still can't see a beaver.

'Which one?'

'The beaver in drag, there.' He points more forcefully, as if a beaver in drag is the most obvious and normal thing in the world. I look again. And there it is. A small, happy-faced beaver, wearing lipstick and a short green dress. It is a little odd, to be honest.

'Was it like that when it was shot?' I say.

'No. I think they dressed it up to make it look pretty afterwards. A beaver wouldn't be dressed like that in the woods.'

I say, 'Right.'

'Yep, this is a hunter's bar. Full of trophies. Everything you see around you is the result of hunting in this area.'

Now, I'm not really a fan of hunting. I don't see the point, when it's just for sport. And what always annoys me is the fact that hunters will claim it's a noble art. A fair fight between man and beast. As if it's arm-wrestling or something. Usually, they'll forget to mention that they've got a high-powered rifle and they're a quarter of a mile away. It's a huge advantage. You may as well challenge a swan at *Boggle*. Or race a bee to Glasgow, but use a car. At the same time, though, there was something strangely impressive about this display of marble-eyed heads. I scanned the room again.

A boar. A ram. A bear. An elk. A moose. An eagle. A tiny bi-plane. A canoe.

All there because of man's love of hunting. All there because of instinct, and guns, and . . .

Hang on.

A bi-plane? A *canoe*?

'Eric?'

'Yeah.'

'What about the bi-plane and the canoe? Are *they* a result of hunting?'

'The what?'

'The tiny bi-plane and the large yellow canoe. How did *they* get here?'

Eric strains to turn round and look where I am pointing. He sees them, and makes a small 'hmm' noise.

'Well, to tell you the truth I've never really noticed them before.'

Eh?

'You've never really noticed . . . a bi-plane in a bar?'

He shakes his head.

'Even though you've been in here virtually every day of your life?'

'Nope,' he says firmly. 'Never noticed them.'

I look back at the bi-plane and Eric goes back to staring straight in front of him. Clearly, this is some kind of cover-up. Clearly, Eric and his

76

pals have shot down a bi-plane and a canoe, have known it is wrong, but still can't resist hanging them up in their local bar as trophies. I decide to keep quiet. Who knows what could happen to a man out here? I suddenly have visions of the next tourist passing through Wallace taking a seat at the bar and being talked through the trophies.

'That's an elk . . . that's a bear . . . that's a specky British bloke who got curious about the bi-plane . . . that's a beaver dressed as Shirley Bassey . . . that's a man with six breasts . . .'

I decide to move tables quietly.

4.50pm
It hasn't been a brilliant move.

'There's nothing better than picking the hair away from a wound you've just made,' says a man named John, instantly winning a medal for the Worst Sentence Anyone Ever Said To Me.

I'm suddenly not sure this is the bar for me. I have come in search of the Centre of the Universe, and now I want to vomit on John's arm. All around me are men. Real men. Men with guns. Men who shoot things. Men who kill. And so I take a sip of my pint, and I say 'yeah'. And I nod. And then John goes quiet. And so I say . . .

'There's nothing better than making your own hamburger, either.'

It is a desperate attempt to fit in. To show I too am a hunter and a gatherer. That my army jacket and cowboy shirt say KILLER rather than TOPMAN. John doesn't say anything. One or two people look over at me. I try and explain.

'You know. Better than buying one. You can put what vegetables you like on it, and . . .'

I take another sip.

'. . . you can decide on how much ketchup you want on it, or if you even want ketchup at all. Or mustard, or whatever.'

I nod to myself and take another sip. No one really says anything. So I say . . .

'But obviously picking the hair out of a wound is better than that.'

I decide not to ask John what the Centre of his Universe is, because I am afraid the answer will terrify me. I go for a walk.

4.58pm

Bollocks. I can't get in to see the stoplight. I

have never wanted to see a stoplight as much as this. I will just have to try and imagine what it looks like.

5.00pm
I bump into Greg again on the high street. I'm looking at a sign that says:

NO BICYCLES, SKATEBOARDS OR ROLLER SKATES ON SIDEWALK

'It's funny how you're not allowed to pop on a pair of roller skates,' I say, 'but you're allowed to drive a snowmobile wherever you like.'

'It's good for tourism,' says Greg. He's drinking coffee from a Centre of the Universe mug. 'We need all the tourists we can get. They get a kick out of the fact they can drive their snowmobile through town.'

'And the stoplight,' I say, sadly. 'I bet when people get to see that, it's a pretty amazing day.'

And then Greg remembers something.

'We're actually going to open up the haunted mines soon,' he says, excitedly. 'As a tourist attraction!'

'Wow. Are they really haunted?'

'Sure,' says Greg. 'And it'll be a great chance for people to learn about the history of the mines, while also having some fun with ghosts. Do you want to see them? I can get them to open up the mines for you. You have to see the mines.'

'You don't have to do that—'

'Come and see the haunted mines!'

'Are they *really* haunted?'

'Sure!'

'They're not, are they?'

'No.'

9 Gold, ghosts and golf at the centre of the universe

5.20pm

Greg has had his good friend drive us out to the haunted mines. I love the fact that you can turn up in a town in order to do one thing, and end up doing quite another. In this case, ghost mining. We are wearing bright yellow hard-hats. Apparently we have to be careful as there is a lynx on the loose in the mine. Also, there are dozens of chipmunks as well. Once news gets out, I imagine every single bloke in the 1313 club will be up here in minutes with spears and chipmunk cannons.

There is great excitement as we walk through the low entrance. At the moment, these mines are just narrow and damp corridors, with the odd lift taking you underground. But soon, I am told, they will be Wallace's number one tourist attraction. Even better than the stoplight, or the Centre of the Universe manhole cover.

'You know, they used to call Wallace "the

richest little city in the world",' says Greg's friend. 'The Gold Rush started just twenty miles to the north of here. And also,' she points to the ceiling, 'right here is where we'll have all the glowing slimy spiders' eggs, which we made with balloons and hair gel.'

'Nice,' I say. 'So Wallace was properly rich, then?'

'Yup. They used to call Wallace "The Silver Capital of the World". We've produced nearly two billion ounces of silver over the years. Oh! And right here is a fake wall which Greg will stand behind and moan as people walk by.'

I love the fact that a formerly serious scientist will soon be spending his afternoons in a hard-hat standing behind walls making scary moaning sounds.

'And right here is where a dummy dressed as a miner will spin above people's heads as we play chilling music,' said Greg, pointing at the ceiling. 'It's going to be fun!'

There was barely enough room to swing a cat, let alone spin a miner. But I nodded my head in approval, which is trickier than it sounds when you're wearing a hard-hat.

'And just behind you is where giant rocks will fall on people's heads.'

I looked behind me. I didn't see the appeal.

'Giant rocks? Why?'

'To show them what a cave-in would be like.'

'Not *real* giant rocks, though?'

'No. Fake ones. Ones we got from the movie set.'

'Which movie set?'

'A movie called *Dante's Peak* was filmed here.'

A *movie!* I was suddenly quite excited. I'm not saying mines are boring. I'm just saying there's a reason we keep them underground.

'Is that the volcano movie?' I said. 'The one starring Pierce Brosnan? The one where a long-quiet volcano suddenly erupts with terrible force? The one where we have to ask ourselves . . . will the world ever be the same, when the silent monster unleashes its fury?'

'That's the one,' said Greg's friend, proudly. 'Filmed right here in Wallace!'

'"The richest little city in the world"!' I say. "The Silver Capital of the World"!'

'Oh!' says Greg's friend. 'I forgot one. "The Home of the Silver Dollar". They used to call it that, too.'

'So what do they call it now that there's so much less mining?'

Greg and his friend looked at me like I was stupid.

'The Centre of the Universe.'

Oh yeah.

5.47pm

Back in town, I have started to look at Wallace in an entirely new light. How exciting to think that Pierce Brosnan himself walked these very streets, looking all cool and Irish. Once Greg had seen my excitement, he told me with a smile that Lana Turner herself was born in Wallace. In fact, her father ran the local dry cleaners. Lana Turner! Herself! She lived here until she was five, in a little house up the road.

When she returned, the Mayor declared a holiday in her honour!

Lana Turner! Lana Turner and me! Both with our own public holidays in Wallace!

'How d'you like *that*?' said Greg. 'People round here are kind of proud of that.'

'They should be!' I say. 'Lana Turner herself!'

And I shake my head a little to show disbelief.

It is only when Greg walks away that I admit to myself that I have no idea who Lana Turner is.

5.49pm

It has stopped raining.

5.50pm

It has started raining again.

6pm

I feel as if I should get to grips with Wallace's history. So I am being led around the top floor of a former brothel by an elderly gentleman doing a speech. We are completely alone. Apart from some shop dummies in odd positions and saucy clothing.

'The Oasis was the last brothel to close, in 1988,' he says.

'*1988?*' I say. 'There were brothels here until 1988?'

'Uh-huh.'

'I thought we were talking about cowboy times!'

'We still get cowboys round here.'

The man made a sweeping gesture with his arm as he showed me the living quarters. It was an odd piece of theatre.

'The girls left in such a hurry that they left a lot of their possessions behind. This place is exactly as it was in 1988.'

'Except for the dummies,' I say.

'Yeah, they weren't here. Just girls. And men.'

Just above the man's head is a sign that says:

IN GOD WE TRUST. EVERYONE ELSE PAYS UP FRONT!

I look at it and laugh a little, but then I worry he thinks I'm laughing at his hair, so we move on.

'This was a town where men used to out-number women 200–1. That's a lot of men. So every two weeks, a busload of women would arrive and start working in Wallace. Then two weeks later they'd get back on the bus and some new ones would arrive.'

'But wasn't this illegal? What did the police think?'

'Well, the police preferred not to know about it. The girls were good to the town. They had quite a lot of respect.'

I looked over and saw an odd uniform hanging on a door.

'What's that? A cheerleader outfit or something?'

'Brass band,' said the man.

I looked at it again. 'That's quite a specific thing to want someone to wear. You'd have to really *love* the tuba.'

'You see, the girls worked at night, and slept during the day. Now this isn't a big town, so when band practice started it was quite noisy for them. So the girls said they'd buy the band new uniforms, if they promised to practise elsewhere.'

'Really? And they did?'

'Uh-huh.'

'So why did they shut down?'

'Well, there was a story that a local politician had agreed to go easy on the houses in exchange for $25,000.'

'Ah.'

'And some people didn't like the fact that the brothels were so accepted. Once, during the final of the big college football game, there was a whole half-time display promoting the brothels.'

'Really? What, like with dancing and stuff?'

'It had the works. And then when they shut 'em down, the students unrolled a forty-foot banner which said GIVE WALLACE BACK ITS HOUSES. Well, that was probably a bit much for some.'

He sighed.

'Yup. It's a pity. They were great girls. So . . . where are *you* from?'

'London.'

'London!' he says, but that appears to be all he has to say on the matter, so I look around the room. I notice that the women who worked here liked peanut butter and *Vogue*.

And the man says, 'Hey! I just thought . . . come downstairs. I *have* something for you . . .'

6.30pm
It was a coin.

Another one.

This one has a picture of the Oasis on it, and is in honour of *100 Years of Service* to the town of Wallace.

The man was very generous to give it to me, but my pockets are starting to feel very heavy indeed.

6.38pm
I was buying a Mars bar and some water from the garage down the road.

'So what is there to do around here?' I ask the man behind the counter. He has just told me that the centre of his universe is his dog.

'Well, what do you *like* doing?' he said. 'Do you like mountain biking?'

'Um . . . I've not really done much of that, no.'

'How about ATVs?'

'ATVs?'

'All terrain vehicles. You like them?'

'I'm not very big on ATVs, I'm afraid.'

'You could go for a long walk.'

'I'm a bit tired.'

The man folded his arms and said 'hmm'.

'You know if it was snowing,' he said, 'you could go skiing. There's some wonderful ski places around here.'

I nodded, and said 'damn', like I'd have been straight up a hill and down again if you'd given me the chance.

Suddenly he had an idea.

'There's a golf course over in Silver Valley!'

It sounded like the worst idea of the lot. Golf is not my game. But I decided to look all pleased so he would feel like he'd really helped me.

'Brilliant! Well, thanks for your help.'

'So you like golf, huh? We found something that you like to do! A golf fan!'

'Yes! Ha ha. Thank you. That's great.'

I took my change and started to walk out the door.

'What's your handicap?' he said.

I pretended to think about it.

'Probably my swing.'

It is lucky I am so quick on my feet. He could have caught me out there.

6.49pm
I notice that the Old Smokehouse looks rather inviting.

10 Crime and midgets at the centre of the universe

7pm

I am sitting in the Old Smokehouse drinking a coffee. Next to me is a man named Marc. He is a logger. He is wearing a Guinness cap and drinking a beer.

The centre of his universe is 'work'. We've been talking about crime in Wallace.

'The mayor told you right,' he says. 'There's no crime in Wallace. If you want crime, you've come to the wrong place.'

The man sitting between us, who neither of us have spoken to yet, grunts in agreement.

'I don't want crime,' I say. 'I know very few people who do.'

'We don't lock our doors here. You don't need to. Trust is what we have. Hell, I don't even take my car keys with me.'

'Where do you leave them?'

'In my car,' he says. 'I leave my keys in my car.'

'Really? What, in the ignition?'

'Yep.'

'Where's your car right now?' I say, in slight disbelief.

'It's the tan pick-up down the street. Keys are in the ignition. My chequebook is on the floor. My CDs are all over the back seat.'

He smiles at me, and I smile at him. How cool is this? Imagine not worrying. Imagine not *needing* to worry. And then the man sitting between us very suddenly finishes his drink. He walks out the door and down the street, in the direction of Marc's pick-up.

I lock eyes with Marc.

And then Marc gets up and stands by the door. He's making sure that bloke isn't nicking his car.

7.06pm
I have just realised that if nobody in Wallace bothers locking their doors, there is very little point in giving me the keys to the city.

7.08pm
Marc the logger has just flicked through my notebook. He stops about halfway through.

'What's that?' he says pointing at a doodle.

'That's a man with six breasts,' I say.

'Oh yeah,' says Marc.

We have another drink.

7.30pm
Greg has arranged for me to visit a friend of his by the name of Len. Len has lived here for a few years. He bought a house overlooking the town for $4500 in 1998. The only problem was the empty house next door. He wanted to find out who owned it, so went to the library, where it turned out that *he* did. His $4500 had also

bought him two other places as well. He was told that if he wanted to get rid of the old house, he should buy a keg of beer and invite the fire department round. He did.

One of the houses next to his is Lana Turner's old house. We are up in Lana Turner's attic, where Len keeps a tiny ping-pong table and some huge plastic rocks he nicked from the set of *Dante's Peak*. I hold one. It is about the size of a beachball. It is very realistic.

I find out that Lana Turner was nominated for an Oscar. She also starred in *Falcon's Crest*, and when she died in 1995 she left behind a load of fans.

'So . . . impressed?' says Len.

'Yes,' I say, handing the rock back to him. 'It's very realistic.'

7.49pm

I am enjoying just wandering around Wallace, seeing what happens. I ask a man who looks like he's come straight out of a book of film extras if he was in *Dante's Peak*. We are standing on the street corner opposite the Centre of the Universe.

'Yup,' he says. 'Or my feet were. They filled

the screen for a second or so.'

'Your feet did?'

'Well, one of my feet did.'

'That's still pretty cool,' I say. 'What was your foot doing?'

'Running. We spent most of our time running.'

'Were lots of people from Wallace in the film?'

'Most of the people in Wallace were in it. Everyone made some money. But like I say, most of it was running. We had a big screening here in town. Everyone came along and cheered everything they recognised. Especially when things got destroyed!'

We laugh.

'Did anyone cheer your foot?'

'There's some disagreement as to whose foot that was. Someone else claimed it was their foot, but it wasn't. It was my foot.'

He looks slightly hurt when he says this, so I make a serious face and nod, so he knows I believe him.

The centre of his universe is 'family'.

He introduces me to a friend of his named Ed.

8.03pm

'Never call a midget a midget,' says Ed, standing outside a bar, having a smoke. I've asked him what lessons he's learned since living in the Centre of the Universe, and that's what he's said. Never call a midget a midget.

'Those little guys, they don't like being called little guys. Or dwarves. Or midgets. You gotta call them "little people". I know that now, because I got myself in trouble one time.'

'Why?' I say. 'What did you say to a little person?'

'I didn't know I had to call him a little person. I didn't know *what* to call him. I panicked.'

'What did you call him?'

'I called him a gnome.'

'A *gnome?*'

'I called him a gnome,' says Ed, taking a drag. 'Yuh. I called him a gnome.'

'How did he react, when you called him a gnome?'

'He looked a little pissed.'

I nod my head.

'That's gnomes for you,' he adds and stubs out his cigarette.

11   Fire and brimstone at the centre of the universe

8.06pm

I decide to go into the bar. I notice that many of the men sitting around the bar not only have a bottle of beer on the go – but a shot of something, too. I don't know what it is and I'm not about to ask. The men all turn out to be hunters, in town from Cincinnati. One of the younger hunters turns an offer of a refill down. I see him point to me and say, 'Give it to that guy, if he wants it.'

The barman looks over at me and holds up the shot glass. I have no idea what he's going to fill it with. I nod, though, and say 'thank you'.

'Keep this quiet,' he says to me.

I promise I will, which is why I haven't told you the name of the bar.

'This is good stuff . . .' he says.

I take a slug. It is indeed good stuff. On a cold day like today, it fairly warms up the stomach.

I look around the bar. Everyone seems happy. There is a sign to my right which says: 'Some people get wet, while others walk in the rain.' It might be the drink I've just had, but it strikes me as the wisest thing I've ever read.

The barman brings me another beer and refills my shot glass.

I thank him and knock back about half of it.

'What *is* this stuff?' I ask.

'Moonshine. Genuine moonshine.'

Hang on. I've *heard* of moonshine. They called it that because it was made at night, when no one could see them doing it. Oh! Because it's *illegal!* It's made from basically anything you can find, and isn't it supposed to be . . . a health hazard? An *illegal health hazard?*

No. Surely not.

'That,' says the barman, pointing at my glass, 'is 160% proof.'

Actually, yes, I think it probably is.

'Wow . . .' I say. 'But it tastes pretty smooth . . .'

'Going down, yeah. But you wait a few minutes . . . wait for The Burn . . .'

'I think I've had The Burn,' I say. 'I felt all warm and tingly.'

'Oh . . . yeah . . . "warm and tingly" . . . you've probably already had it.'

8.26pm
Oh. Ooh. What's *that?*

8.28pm
JESUSCHRISTALMIGHTYWHAT'SGOINGON???

8.29pm
Breathe. Breathe. Wipe your eyes and your nose and just breathe. Breathe through your face.

8.31pm
I have just had The Burn. The *Burn!* Turns out 'warm and tingly' was quite a poor description.

I have started to hiccup. You could light each hiccup and power a small car for nine months.

I need the toilet but I am afraid to go. I feel a fire safety officer should be present. Even my sweat is probably 160% proof right now, and the last thing Wallace needs is another Great Fire. Suppose I somehow miss the urinal and there's a man wearing flammable fabrics nearby? Who knows what could happen?

Also, resources are probably quite low here at the moment, what with that small fire being under investigation.

Overall, it is just too risky.

I stumble out of the bar.

8.33pm
The doors in Wallace are very hard to open and shut. And the pavements suddenly seem very tricky. What a strange town.

It is not because I am drunk.

8.34pm
What is *with* these *pavements?*

8.35pm
Goodness! Leaning up against a window, I notice that a man named Jimi Hendrix is selling a house in Wallace for $42,000. I don't think Jimi Hendrix is his real name. I think his real name is Jim Hendrikson, like it says on the sign in the shop. But that's what the poster in his window says. Jimi Hendrix. It would be a very strange career move if it *was* Jimi Hendrix. To go from rocking the world with his excitable guitar to faking his death. And then

moving to Wallace where he would sell tiny houses for $42,000. But we must not judge him if this turns out to be the case. Perhaps I will find Elvis working in one of the antique shops with the man with the huge beard. And maybe the man with the huge beard is actually Santa. Maybe Santa couldn't get any elves, so he got an Elvis instead. Maybe Jimi Hendrix is an Elvis.

Now that I think about it, I probably *am* quite drunk.

8.38pm
I down a bottle of water at speed. I want to have a nap and a curry but my time in Wallace is running out. I have enjoyed my day, but I should really try and enjoy all of it.

I press on. I ask a woman on a bike what the centre of her universe is. But it is dark, I stink of booze and she cycles off. Even if she had told me I would probably have forgotten her reply anyway.

8.57pm
I am eating some food very quickly. I don't know what it is but it has meat in it which is all

I care about right now. Even what John said about hair and wounds couldn't put me off.

But then it does, so I start on the chips.

12 Phoning home from the centre of the universe

9.25pm
Pavements pretty easy again now.

I try and make a phone call home using a payphone near the garage. But I realise as I pick up the receiver that there is a huge time difference. Everyone I know will have been asleep for hours. I suppose this is what happens when you travel through time and space to get to the Centre of the Universe. It never happened on *Star Trek*, though, did it? You never saw Spock picking up a payphone on some distant planet to ring another Vulcan and then think, 'Actually, better not, he's probably in bed by now.' You never saw them all winding their watches back after entering hyper-space. You'd think they'd be jetlagged all the time.

Also, the only bloody coins I've got on me are a 75th Anniversary coin, a Centre of the Universe coin, a Silver Capital of the World coin and an Oasis Rooms coin. None of them would fit even if I wanted them to.

Annoyed and woozy, I go for a brisk walk around Wallace.

10.15pm
I am back in the 1313 Club, where I have just turned down the offer of more moonshine. Greg has just walked in.

'This place used to be the roughest bar in town,' he says. 'For years it had plywood windows. The guy who ran it didn't see the point in having glass windows. Too many people kept getting thrown through them.'

I looked around. It didn't look rough any more. After all, there was a beaver in drag on the windowsill.

'But Wallace isn't like that any more, is it?' I say. 'It seems that all is peaceful at the Centre of the Universe. I have seen precisely zero men being thrown through windows.'

'It's the most friendly place in America.'

'That's nice.'

'Well, that's the way it *has* to be. That's the way the Centre of the Universe *should* be.'

'How do you mean?'

'The thing about Wallace is, you *have* to get

on with each other. You can't hide like you can hide in a city. You have to deal with everybody who lives here – every kind of person. We only have 960 people. So you talk to them all. From the richest person, to the town drunk. You don't ignore anyone. You can't. If you have a disagreement with someone, the whole town hears about it. You can't hide from it. You have to face it head on. And because of that, people tend to be on their best behaviour. You don't want to make anyone else's life difficult. And also you don't want people talking about what a jerk you are.'

This seemed to me to be quite a good way to live.

'The thing is,' said Greg, taking a sip from his beer, 'this *is* your whole universe . . .'

10.54pm
While Greg pops to the toilet, I think about what he's just said. I guess if you know everybody in town, that can be a bit like knowing everyone in the world. Especially for someone like Joseph, who's never really left town. I guess whether he knows it or not, Wallace *is* the Centre of the Universe for him.

11.01pm
'Can I ask you something, Greg?'
'Sure.'
'What's the Centre of the Universe for *you*?'
'Hmm?'
'I've asked almost everyone else today. I just thought I'd ask you. Some people have said friends. Others have said family. So what's the centre of *your* universe?'

Greg thinks about it for a second.

'I guess Wallace. Wallace is the centre of my universe. To me, it *is* the Centre of the Universe.'

'But you've lived elsewhere. You've travelled the world.'

He puts his beer down and looks at me, very seriously.

'It's not the Centre of the Universe just because I live here. Or because someone with a manhole cover in one hand and a speech in the other just *claims* it is. Wallace is all about something more important than that. Think about it. This is a place that has learnt the important lessons in life. It's a place that now values natural beauty over money. It's a place that has learnt from history and has a vision of the future. It's a place of hard work and of pleasure. There might only be five people per square mile, but the spirit of our universe is expanding.

'Life here is simple, not chaotic. It's about the good things. People getting on with one another. Working hard, but having fun. That's what Wallace is about. *That's* why it's the Centre of the Universe. There's nowhere else like it on earth.'

I am taken aback by Greg's beautiful speech. Here is a man who loves where and how he lives. Who is happy and content. Who doesn't want money or status or power – who gave those things up in order to live the way he does. The way he's happiest.

At last, I guess I have concrete proof. Wallace *is* the Centre of the Universe. Maybe not to everyone. Maybe not to me. But to many. And to Greg especially.

'By the way, I have a gift for you . . .' he says. 'It's a book about mining.'

'Oh – thank you,' I say, and I smile.

'You're smiling,' he says.

'Yeah. It's silly. It's just I thought you were about to give me a coin, that's all.'

Greg nods.

'Yes. I have a coin for you also.'

11.39pm

It has stopped raining.

I take my book and my coin, and I thank Greg for the chat. I tell him he's made me consider a manhole cover in a whole new light.

13 Back at the manhole cover at the centre of the universe

11.40pm

It's getting on for midnight, and I'm standing on the manhole cover at the Centre of the Universe.

I look up and I can see the stars. But this time, I don't feel so small. I think about how we're all at the centre of our *own* universes. And that universe expands every time we meet someone new, or learn something we didn't know, or see something we'd never seen. Wallace is the Centre of the Universe for Greg, but I've got my own Centre of the Universe. So do you. It's the people and the places and the things we love. It's that lady's son, or that bloke's dog.

Who really cares where the actual Centre of the Universe is? Who cares if it's sixty billion miles away, or on a small street in Wallace, Idaho? The Centre of the Universe changes every day. It all just depends on who you ask.

I realise I love Wallace, because Wallace loves what it is. OK, so it may be small. It may not be as rich as it once was. But it's a town with imagination. And warmth. It's a town that stood up to the mighty highway, and won. It's a town with its own values – and currency. A town where you can drive a snowmobile but you have to take your roller skates off first. A town where the Prime Minister runs the hotel. A town founded by a Colonel who wasn't even a colonel. A town where they'll hold a funeral . . . for a *stoplight*. Where complete strangers give you coin after coin. Where football half-time shows celebrate the prostitutes. Where for a keg of beer the local fire service will knock down any building you choose. A town that doesn't *mind* being the rainiest town in Idaho, because 'some people get wet, while others walk in the rain'. A town that will make a complete stranger an ambassador with his own public holiday. A town that'll make a novelty manhole cover into a genuine tourist hotspot. A town that says hello.

Today I listened as one or two people told me Wallace's golden age had gone. But like Greg says, was it really so golden? A town of poison and slagheaps? Look at it now. An odd little reminder of what America used to be like, before Starbucks ruled the earth. The old days were the Silver days in all senses of the word. Now Wallace has been promoted. *These* are Wallace's Golden days.

I want to thank Wallace for my day. But I don't know how.

And then I have an idea.

I wander back to my hotel, just as it starts to rain again.

14 Journey back to the centre of the earth again

9am

It is the next morning. In a couple of hours I have to leave Wallace.

As I walk out of my hotel room, I notice that they've left the local paper outside the door. I pick it up and notice something incredible.

I am front page news! *Front page!* There I am! Grinning like an oddball and pointing at a manhole cover!

LONDON MAN VISITS CENTER OF THE
UNIVERSE

Essentially, this is the same as having a page one headline which says:

LOOK! A TOURIST!

Excited, I decide to go and grab some breakfast and read all about me.

FRIDAY, OCTOBER 14, 2005

SHOSHONE
NEWS-PRESS

Visit us online at www.shoshonenewspress.com 50

London man visits Center of the Universe

— Photo by ERIKA KIRSCH

Danny Wallace, of London, flew nearly 5,000 miles to see the Center of the Universe in Wallace, Idaho. He visited with Wallace Mayor Ron Garitone on Thursday and will be leaving Wallace to fly back to London on Friday afternoon.

Wallace made a 12-hour trip from the Center of the Earth

By ERIKA KIRSCH
Staff writer

WALLACE — Danny Wallace

He had to come, he said; the connection between his name and the name of the town that is home to the coveted Center of the

9.18am

It is a great article.

I drink my huckleberry milkshake and read it in depth.

> **WALLACE** – Danny Wallace came from the Centre of the Earth to see the Center of the Universe! Wallace, from London, can see Greenwich, Great Britain, from the windows of his apartment.

Well, it'd be a bit odd if I could see Greenwich, Texas. I'd have to have massive magnifying windows, for a start. People in passenger jets would be able to see me changing.

> This spurred an interest in Wallace and he explored the Internet and came up with the Center of the Universe. The irony is that the Center of the Universe just happened to be a town called Wallace.
>
> He booked a flight and emailed Wallace Mayor Ron Garitone. Garitone admitted he had no idea who Wallace was, but upon meeting him, Garitone was impressed.
>
> 'I'm very fascinated by him,' Garitone said.

'Hopefully I befriended him and I can keep in touch with him.'

I was touched. The mayor is fascinated by me! And he wants to be my friend! Well, I suppose I *am* tremendously enjoyable.

The article goes on to give details of the Mayor's plans for Danny Wallace Day. And it reminds them that I am, in fact, their Ambassador.

I head for City Hall. But there's something I have to do on the way, first.

10.40am
I am back at the Mayor's office.

'Is the Mayor in?' I ask.

'I'm afraid not,' says the lady behind the desk. 'Is it anything I can help you with?'

'I've brought a gift,' I say.

I unveil the small brass plaque I've just had made.

'I went to the computers and engraving shop around the corner. I got them to make this!'

A second lady stands up and says, 'What *is* it?'

'It's an award! I have just started the WALLACE INTERNATIONAL AWARDS. Although I should point out that *I* am the Wallace in that title, not you.'

The first lady took it, and read from it.

'For outstanding international achievements in the field of outstanding international achievements. The town of Wallace is awarded the title of—'

'Finest Little Town in the Universe!'

'Well, isn't that great?' says the second lady, looking genuinely pleased.

'I thought you could put it next to your "Twenty-fourth Best Place to Buy a Second Home" award. I thought it might make up for coming twenty-fourth.'

'Well!' she said. 'Ron will be very happy!'

'Good. Well . . . I'll be off, then.'

'Back to London?'

'Yup.'

But as I leave to go, the second lady calls out, 'Mr Wallace?'

'Yes?'

'I have something for you. A parting gift. I meant to give it to you yesterday. It's something to remember your time here by.'

And she feels around in her handbag, and she pulls something out.

A coin.

I take it, and smile, and say thank you, like it's the first one I've been given. And I walk away from Wallace, with my huge, heavy pockets jangling away.

Epilogue

Dear Staff of the Royal Observatory,

I thought I would let you know that I went to Wallace, Idaho, and I did indeed find out where the Centre of the Universe is.

Please do not worry. You are not merely a worthless speck of dust here by chance in an infinite universe. Which is very nice of me to say, particularly when you consider you still haven't replied to my first email.

What I mean is, maybe you shouldn't be looking through a telescope to find the universal truths that matter.

Anyway, I have written down my findings in a document I have called *Danny Wallace and the Centre of the Universe*, and I will be sending a copy to you shortly. I would appreciate it if you would keep it in the Observatory on permanent display, so that the young may learn from it.

With thanks, and tremendous enjoyment,

Danny Wallace
The Official Ambassador to the (possible) Centre
of the Universe

WORLD BOOK DAY
Quick Reads

Quick Reads are published alongside and in partnership with BBC RaW.

We would like to thank all our partners in the *Quick* Reads project for all their help and support:

Department for Education and Skills
Trades Union Congress
The Vital Link
The Reading Agency
National Literacy Trust

Quick Reads would also like to thank the Arts Council England and National Book Tokens for their sponsorship.

We would also like to thank the following companies for providing their services free of charge: SX Composing for typesetting all the titles; Icon Reproduction for text reproduction; Norske Skog, Stora Enso, PMS and Iggusend for paper/board supplies; Mackays of Chatham, Cox and Wyman, Bookmarque, White Quill Press, Concise, Norhaven and GGP for the printing.

www.worldbookday.com

Quick Reads

BOOKS IN THE *Quick* Reads SERIES

Blackwater	Conn Iggulden
The Book Boy	Joanna Trollope
Chickenfeed	Minette Walters
Cleanskin	Val McDermid
Danny Wallace and the Centre of the Universe	Danny Wallace
Desert Claw	Damien Lewis
Don't Make Me Laugh	Patrick Augustus
The Dying Wish	Courttia Newland
The Grey Man	Andy McNab
Hell Island	Matthew Reilly
How to Change Your Life in 7 Steps	John Bird
I Am a Dalek	Gareth Roberts
I Love Football	Hunter Davies
The Name You Once Gave Me	Mike Phillips
The Poison in the Blood	Tom Holland
Screw It, Let's Do It	Richard Branson
Someone Like Me	Tom Holt
Star Sullivan	Maeve Binchy
The Team	Mick Dennis
The Thief	Ruth Rendell
Winner Takes All	John Francome
Woman Walks into a Bar	Rowan Coleman

**Look out for more titles in the *Quick* Reads
series being published in 2007.**

www.worldbookday.com

FIRST CHOICE BOOKS

If you enjoyed this book, you'll find more great reads on www.firstchoicebooks.org.uk. First Choice Books allows you to search by type of book, author and title. So, whether you're looking for romance, sport, humour – or whatever turns you on – you'll be able to find other books you'll enjoy.

You can also borrow books from your local library. If you tell them what you've enjoyed, they can recommend other good reads they think you will like.

First Choice is part of The Vital Link, promoting reading for pleasure. To find out more about The Vital Link visit www.vitallink.org.uk

RaW

BBC RaW is the BBC's biggest-ever campaign about reading and writing. Find out more online at bbc.co.uk/raw or telephone 08000 150 950.

NEW ISLAND

New Island publishers have produced four series of books in its Open Door series – brilliant short novels for adults from the cream of Irish writers. Visit www.newisland.ie and go to the Open Door section.

SANDSTONE PRESS

In the Sandstone Vista Series, Sandstone Press Ltd publish quality contemporary fiction and non-fiction books. The full list can be found at their website www.sandstonepress.com.